Six-Word Lessons for
COMPELLING SPEECHES

100 Lessons to Deliver
Speeches that Move
Your Audience

Mary Waldmann

Published by Pacelli Publishing
Bellevue, Washington

Six-Word Lessons for Compelling Speeches

Six-Word Lessons for Compelling Speeches

All rights reserved. No part of this book may be reproduced or transmitted in any form or by any means, electronic or mechanical including photocopying, recording or by any information storage or retrieval system, without the written permission of the publisher, except where permitted by law.

Limit of Liability: While the author and the publisher have used their best efforts in preparing this book, they make no representation or warranties with respect to accuracy or completeness of the content of this book. The advice and strategies contained herein may not be suitable for your situation. Consult with a professional when appropriate

Copyright © 2014, 2017 by Mary Waldmann

Published by Pacelli Publishing
9905 Lake Washington Blvd. NE, #D-103
Bellevue, Washington 98004
Pacellipublishing.com

ISBN-10: 1-933750-42-1
ISBN-13: 978-1-933750-42-2

Author photo by Yuen Lui Photography
Cover photo by 123RF/hxdbzy
Cover and interior design by Pacelli Publishing

Introduction

The ability to make an effective and dynamic presentation is a very important professional skill. And the ability to make a good toast or tell a joke can be a wonderful social asset. Yet when quizzed about what they fear most, people inevitably list public speaking near the top, right along with death, paralysis and terrorist attack. Why? We fear doing badly or appearing foolish in front of others. We may avoid professional presentations if we think we won't live up to expectations.

Six-Word Lessons for Compelling Speeches gives you all the tools needed to do a great job in front of an audience. If you follow this advice and use the techniques described, you can be confident in your presentations and you'll be an effective and interesting speaker. As you develop your skills, interacting with an audience can actually become fun.

Even if your speeches are drafted by others in your organization, you need to practice these tips to make the speech your own and to deliver it well.

The information in the book is based on the author's years of experience as a public speaker, as well as teaching hundreds of business leaders and government officials to be effective in their oral presentations.

Follow the book's advice, and you can give effective and dynamic presentations, and enjoy doing it.

Dedication

For Raymond Waldmann, my beloved husband and best editor.

Table of Contents

Questions You Need to Immediately Ask 7

How to Write an Effective Speech 19

Working Easily with a Written Text 31

Practicing Your Presentation Will Improve It 43

Prepare in Advance for Your Speech 55

When You're Ready to Begin Speaking 67

Special Tips for Using Visual Aids 79

How to Deal Well with Questions 91

Some Advice for Special Speaking Situations 103

How to Learn from Your Experience 115

Six-Word Lessons for Compelling Speeches

Questions You Need to Immediately Ask

Why was I asked to speak?

If you don't know, find out why they asked you in particular. Are you a recognized expert on this subject? Did someone recommend you? Is the topic related to your job responsibility? What do they know about you?

— # What topic will I speak on?

Find out exactly what the group wants you to address. This will help you define your purpose and message. You can tell them what *you* want to say in addition to what *they* want to hear about, but don't stray too far from their request.

When's the speech going to occur?

Obviously, you need to know the date and time. Think about your presentation in the time context. If you'll be speaking after a meal or late in the day, you'll need to be particularly dynamic to keep the audience attentive and focused.

How long should my speech be?

Always know how long you are expected to speak and honor that time limit. Find out if that time includes a Question and Answer (Q&A) session or if additional time is allotted for that. If you speak too long, you'll irritate the program planner, the audience and any subsequent speakers.

Who will be in the audience?

Find out something about your audience. Who are they and what do they have in common? How much do they already know about your subject? If your presentation is too technical and difficult for the audience, you'll lose them. Conversely, you don't want to talk down to them.

Who else is on the program?

Will there be other speakers on the program? If so, what topics are they addressing? What is the order of speakers? Does another speaker hold views opposing yours? If that speaker precedes you, you'll need to be prepared to rebut their arguments when it's your turn to speak.

Will there be a Q&A session?

If time will be allowed for questions, how long will it be? Will people ask questions from the floor, or submit them in writing? If you've received sufficient information in advance, you should have some idea what type of questions you'll be asked, and that will help you to give informed answers.

8

Where will the speech be given?

Know the exact location of the venue. If necessary, ask where you should park. What is the room layout—classroom, theater seating, or something else? You don't want to be speaking in front of a large distracting window. If you have preferences in how the room is set up, it's OK to voice them.

Is someone going to introduce me?

If someone will be introducing you, you may want to provide them in advance with a suggested introduction. That will improve the odds that the audience hears exactly what *you* want them to hear.

10

Will there be audio/visual equipment available?

If you plan to use audio/visual aids, find out what equipment is available. Will you be responsible for running it, or will someone else be willing to do it? If you need a flip tablet or easel for your presentation, be sure to request it.

Six-Word Lessons for Compelling Speeches

Six-Word Lessons for Compelling Speeches

How to Write an Effective Speech

Start by defining purpose and message.

What is the purpose of your speech? Do you want to inform or persuade? What message do you want to impart? Try to summarize your central message in one to three sentences. If you can't do that, you need to further refine the message. Keep it concise and to-the-point.

Keep in mind your audience members.

As you write your presentation, always remember who is in the audience. Write and speak to their level of technical knowledge and understanding. Be prepared to address any biases or disagreements with your message that they may already hold.

Come up with a great opening.

Your first sentence should always be an attention-grabber. A question, whether real or hypothetical, can be a great opening. A story relating to your message can also grab your audience from the beginning. A short joke or quip can be effective, but only if it relates to your topic.

14

Be prepared to develop your story.

Once you have a key message, develop that story with additional information, anecdotes, and real-life examples. Keep the presentation lively and interesting. Use colorful examples and language. You have to be entertaining as well as informative.

Summarize points as you go along.

Remember that the audience doesn't have an outline of your speech. It helps them to organize the information and remember it if you enumerate your points and give a one-sentence summary of each point before proceeding to the next.

How to be effective using humor.

Humor helps an audience to remember, but your humor must be central to the message or you run the risk they will remember the joke but not your point. You can use a joke or humorous story to reinforce a point, but keep it short.

Always avoid irony, puns or sarcasm.

Irony and sarcasm can easily be misunderstood. Additionally, they may alienate some members of your audience. For those reasons, it's a good idea to avoid sarcastic and ironic attempts at humor altogether. You can, however, point out ironies in a situation.

18

Avoid saying anything that could offend.

Avoid saying anything even remotely racist, sexist or ageist. Also avoid casual or irreverent references to God. I once described my reaction to an event as an "Oh, God!" moment and was subsequently chastised by a member of the audience. Note to self--don't make that mistake again!

Be prepared to answer some questions.

Even if there's no formal Q&A following your presentation, you should always be prepared for questions that may arise. You might need to answer some clarifying questions as you go along. If you've done your homework and know your subject, you should be able to predict the likely questions.

End with a great closing sentence.

The opening and closing of your speech are the most crucial parts for getting your message across. Always alert the audience that you're at the end by saying something like, "In conclusion…" or, "The final message I'd like to leave you with is…" Make the closing snappy and attention-worthy.

Six-Word Lessons for Compelling Speeches

Working Easily with a Written Text

What to use? Text or outline?

Decide what written aid you'll need. Are you more comfortable with an outline, bullet points or a full text? If specific wording is important for legal or policy reasons, you may want to use a full text. Some speakers simply prefer using a full text. However, be prepared to deliver it, rather than just reading from the pages.

22

Use full-size paper, not index cards.

You want to maintain as much eye contact with your audience as possible. Index cards force you to look further down and detract from good eye contact. For the same reason, leave a healthy margin at the bottom of each page.

Double or triple space the text.

Your text or outline will be much more readable if you double or triple space it. The number of pages you end up with really doesn't matter, so use spacing to make your notes or text as easy to read as possible.

Use a font that's easily readable.

Use a font that is clear and easy to read. Avoid excessive serif. Calibri and Arial are good typefaces for those who want it completely sans serif. Cambria, Times and Times New Roman are good choices for those who prefer a little serif.

Don't hyphenate words at line endings.

If you hyphenate a word at the end of a line you will tend to automatically pause a bit when you move from line to line. A pause between syllables isn't appropriate and makes it apparent that you're reading, so avoid hyphenation.

Don't break paragraphs at page bottom.

For the same reason, don't break up a paragraph at the end of a page unless a pause at that point is appropriate to the delivery. You want your delivery to flow as naturally as possible, so format the text in a way that allows this.

Underline words you want to emphasize.

Underlining key words will help you put emphasis in the right places. When you see the underlining, it causes you to automatically hit those words a little harder. Reading your text aloud will help you to see which words should be emphasized. But don't overdo it.

28

Slide the pages rather than turning.

When you go to the podium, place your first page to the left and the second page to the right of it. As you finish subsequent pages, slide that page to the left. Flipping the pages over is a visual distraction and makes it more apparent that you are using a text. This is particularly important if your text is on a table instead of a podium.

Try not to carry your text.

You'll look more confident as you go to the podium if you're not carrying a speech text or notes. If possible, place your notes at the podium before you get up to speak. If there is a lower shelf, place your text there. If other speakers precede you, however, don't do it, or they might inadvertently remove your text.

30

Always bring at least two copies.

Always have a spare copy of your speech text or notes. You never know when you may accidentally misplace or damage one prior to your delivery. It's good insurance to have a second copy. If you're accompanied by an assistant or staff member, give them the second copy for safekeeping.

Six-Word Lessons for Compelling Speeches

Practicing Your Presentation Will Improve It

First, read your speech aloud once.

After writing your speech, read it through once aloud. This will help you determine which words need emphasis or where there may be awkward breaks or pauses. If you stumble over a particular word or phrase, change that wording. This is especially important if your speech was drafted by someone else.

Get as much practice as possible.

Practice may not always make perfect, but it will certainly improve your delivery. As soon as you've finished writing the presentation, start practicing it aloud. You'll become familiar with the wording, increasing the odds that you'll use the same wording when you actually speak. This will improve eye contact.

Improve delivery by making a recording.

If you have access to a means of recording your speech, record it and listen critically to the playback. Are you using good vocal dynamics? Are you speaking too slowly or too fast? Are the pauses in the right places?

Practice in front of another person.

If possible, practice in front of another person and ask for their suggestions for improvement. Was the talk interesting? Did it flow naturally? Did you maintain good eye contact? Did you avoid using a monotone delivery? Another person's perspective is always helpful.

Think about where to use gestures.

Gestures can be a very effective visual aid. Use your fingers to enumerate points, e.g., one finger for the first point, two for the second and so on. When you describe something as larger, smaller, higher or lower, let your gestures reinforce the words. Use gestures to emphasize key points.

Always practice using any visual aids.

If you are going to use any visual aids, always practice using them in advance of your speech. If you're writing on a flip tablet, make sure your writing can be seen from the back of the room. If using a laptop make sure that it's working before you begin and that charts, photos or other material are in the proper order.

Always role-play your Q&A in advance.

It's a good idea to have someone role-play the anticipated questions. This makes it more likely that you will remember the response you have prepared. This is particularly important if you expect tough questions. Major political candidates always do this before debates—take a lesson from them.

Use active visualization to improve delivery.

When you visualize an activity, brain neurons fire in the same order as when you actually perform it. So use this technique to improve your speech delivery. Closing your eyes and visualizing your presentation from beginning to end can be an effective method of practice. Do it before you go to sleep at night.

Memorize your opening and closing sentences.

Your opening and closing must have impact. You want to have unbroken eye contact for at least your first and final sentences. Memorize those lines so you can deliver them without looking down at your notes. Memorizing the full first and last paragraphs is even better.

Don't practice the day you're speaking.

It's not a good idea to practice your speech right before delivery. You may find yourself, midway through the presentation, wondering if you've already said something or not. Do your practicing in advance of the event day.

Six-Word Lessons for Compelling Speeches

Prepare in Advance for Your Speech

Will you be using any handouts?

If you're going to be using handouts, make sure you print a few more than you anticipate needing. If you're showing complex charts or diagrams, it's a good idea to provide the same information on handouts that audience members can take with them.

What is the appropriate dress code?

Depending on the audience and event, plan your attire appropriately. When in doubt, go more formal rather than more casual. Avoid distracting prints on ties or dresses. Bright colors, however, help attract visual attention. Red can be a good choice. Whatever you wear, make sure it's wrinkle-free.

Give some thought to good grooming.

If you need a haircut, get one. If you won't be wearing a jacket, especially in warm weather, be sure to use antiperspirant. Underarm stains are a distraction and make you look really nervous. Men, if you're prone to five o'clock shadow and your presentation is late in the day, try to squeeze in an additional shave.

Plan to arrive a little early.

Get to the venue at least 20 minutes prior to the program beginning. Check the layout of the room. Is there a microphone? What kind? Get your visual aids and/or handouts organized. If possible, meet the person who will introduce you. If you're going to place your text or notes at the podium, do so now.

Get enough sleep the night before.

You can't do your best job on a presentation if you're short of sleep so plan the previous day's schedule accordingly. Don't plan a late night prior to the presentation day. And you don't want to be hung over, so avoid partying the night before.

Meet the people in the audience.

Arriving early may also allow you to get acquainted with some of the audience members. Meeting them in advance will give you at least a few friendly faces in the audience and help to relax you. You may also be able to refer to a question someone asked you earlier during the body of your presentation.

Don't be afraid to plant questions.

Sometimes the Q&A begins and nobody wants to ask the first question. If you're talking to an audience member before the speech, don't be afraid to suggest a question and ask them to pose it at the appropriate time. That way you won't have an awkward lengthy pause before questions begin to flow.

Always avoid any alcohol or caffeine.

Alcohol will not relax you, it will simply deaden your performance. Avoid it even if there's a preceding cocktail period or wine at a dinner event. Alcohol, as well as coffee and tea, have an astringent effect and may give you dry mouth. Caffeine will make you jittery, which increases that nervous feeling.

Remember: restroom, zippers, buttons and mirror.

During the time prior to your presentation, take time to visit the restroom. Make sure that all zippers and buttons are fastened, and there's nothing caught in your teeth. This seems obvious, but you'd be amazed how many people forget to check ... and it shows.

50

Know that you are the expert.

If you've done your homework and prepared well, you should be able to approach the event with confidence. Remind yourself that you are the expert or you wouldn't have been invited to speak. You are there because you have information or views that the audience wants.

Six-Word Lessons for Compelling Speeches

When You're Ready to Begin Speaking

Be alert, stand tall, look confident.

The audience makes up to twenty decisions about you before you even begin to speak. Look alert and sure of yourself during any introduction. Stand tall and walk confidently to the podium. Smile at the audience. You want to exude confidence and professionalism from the minute the audience's eyes are on you.

Please listen carefully to the introduction.

Listen carefully to the introduction—even if you wrote it. You'll want to know if there's a quip or reference that you can acknowledge or use as you begin your presentation. If there are honored guests present, you may want to acknowledge them. Thank the introducer by name before you begin your speech.

Take time to adjust the microphone.

If there's a microphone on the podium, make sure you adjust the position to your height before you begin speaking. You look awkward and uncomfortable if you have to lean over or stretch to be easily heard. Keep in mind that the microphone should generally be about a fingers-spread hand length from your mouth.

54

Take a deep breath and begin.

Before you begin speaking, take a deep breath and exhale. This will help to relax and focus you. Also, take a few seconds to scan the audience, making eye contact with individuals before you begin. Unless your subject is grave, give them a smile.

Look at the audience when starting.

Because you've memorized your opening sentence, deliver it while looking directly at the audience. You may instinctively want to look down, so fight the impulse if necessary. First impressions are important and you'll look more like you know what you're talking about if looking up.

56

Speak slowly and take your time.

It takes an audience a little time to absorb what you're saying, so take your time on the delivery. Nervousness and adrenaline often make us speak faster than normal; avoid racing through your presentation. Pause frequently and appropriately so the audience can "catch up."

Remember to maintain some eye contact.

Even if you are reading from a text, it's important to maintain good eye contact. Look at all sections of the room, particularly if it's a wide room or the audience is in a semicircle. Don't just quickly scan the room—take time to make contact with individuals.

58

Look down, look up, and speak.

For the most effective delivery of a text, look down, grab an entire sentence, then look up and deliver it. This takes a little practice, so definitely practice with your text, but it will make your delivery much more effective. You want to be looking at the audience whenever your mouth is moving.

Remember that you must be dynamic.

Never speak in a monotone or you'll lose your audience. Good vocal dynamics are vital. Emphasize the important words. Let your inflection rise at the end of questions, rhetorical or otherwise. But end declarative sentences with a downward inflection.

60

Breathe deeply, look up and conclude.

Just like at the beginning, when you reach your conclusion, take a deep breath and pause before summarizing your message. Remember that you should have memorized the final paragraph, or at least the final sentence, so you can deliver it without looking down.

Six-Word Lessons for Compelling Speeches

Special Tips for Using Visual Aids

Don't rely totally on A/V equipment.

While audiovisuals can enhance a presentation, you shouldn't be totally dependent on them. There's always the chance of a breakdown in electronic equipment. If you are giving a PowerPoint presentation, either have back-up equipment available, or be prepared to give the presentation without visuals.

Always test your equipment in advance.

If you're using electronic equipment, ALWAYS test it in advance. It's very annoying to an audience to have to wait while equipment problems are solved. A delay makes you look less professional. If someone else is operating the equipment, make sure you've run through it with that person in advance.

Always use large print on charts.

If you're using charts or diagrams, make sure they can easily be seen from the back of the room. If you have any doubt, be prepared with handout copies. Keep the wording simple. If you're using a number of charts or diagrams, only "unveil" each one when you're ready to address it.

Use handouts for charts and diagrams.

Even if your diagrams can easily be seen, it's still a good idea to have take-away handouts if they are complicated or numerous. Make sure handouts include your name and contact information in case a member of the audience has a later question.

Don't pass out handouts in advance.

If you pass out handouts in advance, people are likely to be reading them rather than listening to your opening. When possible, don't pass anything out until you reach the appropriate point in your presentation, but do it as quickly as possible. Better yet, wait until the end.

Avoid turning the lights down excessively.

Your facial expressions and body language help to emphasize what you're saying, so don't handicap yourself by turning the lights out. If your A/V requires dimming the lights, keep them as bright as possible. Always begin your talk with full light and have someone bring up the lights for your conclusion.

Don't turn your back when speaking.

If you are writing on an easel flip tablet or chalkboard, don't speak while your back is turned toward the audience. Write down what you need to write, then turn around before addressing the audience.

Cartoons can be effective visual aids.

Cartoons, if they make an appropriate point, can be very effective and memorable visual aids. Well-suited cartoons from sources like *The New Yorker* magazine or *The Far Side*, were some of my favorite methods to illustrate a point.

Don't make your visuals too complicated.

Any visuals, no matter what medium, should always be quickly readable and understandable. Don't make them too complicated. You want the audience to be paying attention to what you have to say, not be busy figuring out the visuals.

70

Don't just read your PowerPoint slides.

If you are delivering a PowerPoint presentation, PLEASE do not just read from it. This is boring. Use illustrations or bullet points which you then address in detail. This way you'll also appear more in command of your information.

How to Deal Well with Questions

When will the questions be asked?

If audience questions are to be held until the conclusion of your remarks, make sure the audience knows that. And when you're approaching the end of the Q&A session, whether because the time is up, or you decide to end it, announce that you're taking the last question.

Roleplay your Q&A session in advance.

If you've done adequate preparation, you should be able to anticipate the questions ahead of time. Write down your replies so you're more likely to remember the specific wording, then practice answering them. This is especially important if you anticipate tough or hostile questions.

Listen with care to the questions.

Avoid the impulse to start framing your answer before you've heard the entire question. Listen to it completely before answering. Look at the questioner while he or she is speaking. If the question isn't clear, ask for clarification before trying to respond.

It's good to repeat the question.

It's always a good idea to repeat the question. This assures that you've understood it and makes it clear to the audience what you're responding to. It's very frustrating to audience members when they haven't heard the question clearly. If it's a lengthy question, you may want to paraphrase it more succinctly.

If you don't know, say so.

If you don't know the answer, always admit it. Don't try to bluff your way through a response. If you need additional information, you can volunteer to get it and give it to the program chairman for dissemination to the audience members at a later date.

Don't explain how to make watches.

Keep your answers concise and to-the-point. If someone asks you the time of day, you don't start by explaining how a watch is made. Similarly, try to avoid giving a lot of background to your response. Only say what's necessary to answer the question completely.

Never catch a "ball of worms."

This is a question which contains multiple parts. If you catch it, you'll find yourself trying to remember the subsequent parts while still addressing the first, or else you'll answer the first and forget what followed. Ask the questioner to break the question apart for you.

Don't accept a negative as true.

This is the "When did you stop beating your wife?" kind of question. Never repeat the negative. Don't say "I never beat my wife." Make a positive statement that rebuts the charge: "I have always treated my wife with the utmost love and respect."

Avoid answering with speculation or characterization.

Don't be drawn into speculating about future events about which you have no complete knowledge. If you have the back-up facts, you can say "If this, then that" but make sure you have the information to back it up. Never make a negative characterization of a third party.

# 80

Relate questions to your central points.

Always try to relate the question to your key points and segue back to your message. Questions can also allow you to further elaborate on a particular point and can serve to reinforce your message. Relate answers to personal experience whenever you can.

Some Advice for Special Speaking Situations

What if there'll be media coverage?

Depending on who you are and the importance of your presentation, you may have media present for your speech. Always find out in advance if you think media representatives might be there. If they will be, have copies of your speech text and/or any handouts available when they arrive. Be sure to include your contact information.

What about hecklers in the audience?

If you anticipate troublemakers, ask your host in advance how they will handle it. Always keep yourself allied with the audience members. Say, "In deference to the audience members who want to hear this presentation, I'm asking you to sit down". And a little humor, properly used, can deflate a heckler.

How to handle an audience speechmaker.

If a questioner is making a speech more than asking a question, again ally yourself with the rest of the audience. Say, "Out of respect to the others who have questions, please get to your question so we can go on." You may have to say it more than once.

What if you lose your place?

This can happen, particularly if you're speaking without detailed notes. A little humor can go a long way. I've on occasion said "I apologize...I think my mind just went to Jamaica and didn't come back. Someone please tell me what I was saying?" Don't be afraid to admit human frailty.

What if you make a misstatement?

If you make a major misstatement of fact, of course you need to correct it. But if you've simply stumbled over a word or phrase, don't stop to correct it. You just draw attention to the mistake. Odds are, the audience will understand what you meant to say.

What to do when emergencies arise.

If an emergency arises, it has to be dealt with. I was once in the middle of my speech when the fire alarm sounded and we evacuated. Twenty minutes later, I had to resume. Begin by summarizing what you said prior to the interruption. If medics have been called, express your concern for the person who's in distress.

If there's an A/V mechanical breakdown

Remember that you should have practiced the A/V to minimize the odds of a problem. If one arises which can be quickly corrected, do so, but if the problem persists, you must be prepared to go on with your presentation sans visuals. This is where handouts come in handy.

88

What if you experience dry mouth?

Even if you've avoided alcohol and caffeine, you may experience a dry mouth as the result of additional adrenaline flow. Try gently biting on the tip of your tongue a couple of times. This causes saliva to flow. If you experience the problem frequently, try a breath mint or hard candy before your presentation.

If you're dealing with stage fright

Even people like Laurence Olivier and Barbra Streisand have experienced stage fright! Don't let it throw you. Take several deep breaths to relax. Use positive self-talk. Remind yourself that you are the expert. Don't say to yourself "I'm scared," rather say, "I'm energized and ready for this speech."

90

Some tips for doing panel presentations

If you're participating in a panel presentation, always know in advance who the other presenters are and what the format will be. Be prepared to hold your own—don't allow one person to dominate. When responding to another panelist's remarks, use that panelist's name. You'll probably be seated, so be sure to sit up straight.

Six-Word Lessons for Compelling Speeches

How to Learn from Your Experience

Take time to analyze your performance.

Once you've made a presentation, never just file or toss the text. Take time to think about how you did. Were you happy with how it went? Did things come up that you hadn't anticipated? Would you do anything differently next time?

Ask other people for their reactions.

If possible, ask someone who was there for a critique. He or she may view the presentation differently than you do. What was it like from the audience perspective? Was your message clear and concise? Were there other things that should have been addressed?

If the presentation was recorded, watch.

Videotape can be your best teacher. If the presentation was recorded, always ask if you can watch it. Even better, get a copy. Was your eye contact good? Was your voice dynamic? Were your gestures appropriate? Did you look confident and authoritative?

94

Did you feel preparation was adequate?

Are there things you realize now that you should have asked or done in advance and didn't? Did you feel like you had practiced enough to be confident and comfortable with the presentation? Was your A/V practice sufficient to avoid glitches? Would additional practice have helped?

Did the Q&A go as expected?

Were there any questions that you hadn't anticipated? Make note of them for the future. This is particularly important for difficult or hostile questions, or ones which required information you didn't have. If you promised to provide follow-up information, make sure you do so.

Focus on what things worked well.

Particularly look at the things that went well. Why did they succeed? You'll want to remember these for the future. Was there a quip that evoked a good response? What questions seemed to generate the greatest interest? Incorporate that information into your next presentation.

Don't beat yourself up over mistakes.

If something went wrong or not as expected, analyze why it didn't work. How can you change it next time? Always try to learn from any mistakes. That's the way to improve your speechmaking abilities over time. But then let it go. Don't obsess about what may have gone wrong.

Will you be repeating the speech?

If you'll be repeating the presentation for another group, it's essential that you have good notes on what worked and what didn't. If you found parts of your text difficult, rewrite them. If you'll be addressing the same group in the future, you'll want a record of your presentation and how it went.

Don't forget post-speech thank-you notes.

If it's appropriate to thank the host organization or the program organizer, by all means do so, particularly if you'd like to be invited back. An e-mail message the next day is OK, but a hand written thank-you note has more impact. You might also ask that person how they felt the presentation went.

100

Look for opportunities to gain experience.

The more often you give speeches or presentations, the more comfortable you'll be with the process. Repetition creates confidence and command of your subject. So look for opportunities to gain further experience. As you do, speaking will become increasingly enjoyable.

About the *Six-Word Lessons Series*

Legend has it that Ernest Hemingway was challenged to write a story using only six words. He responded with the story, "For sale: baby shoes, never worn." The story tickles the imagination. Why were the shoes never worn? The answers are left up to the reader's imagination.

This style of writing has a number of aliases: postcard fiction, flash fiction, and micro fiction. Lonnie Pacelli was introduced to this concept in 2009 by a friend, and started thinking about how this extreme brevity could apply to today's communication culture of text messages, tweets and Facebook posts. He wrote the first book, *Six-Word Lessons for Project Managers*, then started helping other authors write and publish their own books in the series.

The books all have six-word chapters with six-word lesson titles, each followed by a one-page description. They can be written by entrepreneurs who want to promote their businesses, or anyone with a message to share.

See the entire *Six-Word Lessons Series* at 6wordlessons.com

www.ingramcontent.com/pod-product-compliance
Lightning Source LLC
Chambersburg PA
CBHW070643050426
42451CB00008B/287